BUTTERFLY FLUTTERS

Butterfly Flutters

Poems for Spiritual Inspiration
by
MONICA TIMBAL

Adelaide Books
New York/Lisbon
2019

BUTTERFLY FLUTTERS
Poems for Spiritual Inspiration
By Monica Timbal

Copyright © by Monica Timbal
Cover design © 2019 Adelaide Books

Published by Adelaide Books, New York / Lisbon
adelaidebooks.org

Editor-in-Chief
Stevan V. Nikolic

All rights reserved. No part of this book may be reproduced in any manner whatsoever without written permission from the author except in the case of brief quotations embodied in critical articles and reviews.

For any information, please address Adelaide Books
at info@adelaidebooks.org
or write to:
Adelaide Books
244 Fifth Ave. Suite D27
New York, NY, 10001

ISBN-10: 1-949180-92-1
ISBN-13: 978-1-949180-92-3

Printed in the United States of America

To Manu

My joy takes flight
On lightest wings of butterflies.
Words! my flight of fancy-
Of fleeting, colored fireflies.

Dream for me a life of awesome beauty
Dream for me a life of endless love,
A life of soaring aspirations and impeccable design
Dream for me of happiness and victory
Dream me, Self, into eternity.

Earth welcomes her lover, the sky
Secret kisses of delight
In the blushing morning daylight.

Descend again through cosmic spheres
Gathering star dust
According to necessity and fate,
A spark, of heavenly forces
And with divine intent,
Fall down and take on earthly gears
And try a new
The Great Work to perfect and to end
And forever to ascend.

On my eternal journey
I take my joy in life,
I take my rest in death.

Oh, little butterfly, don't despair
Your long sleep in your cocoon
Is preparing you
For the flight of your life.

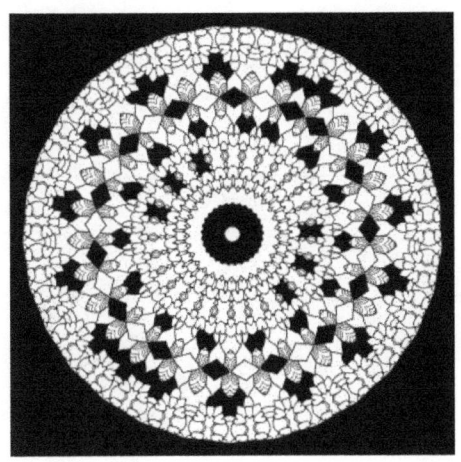

Sweet moon rain down ambrosial dew
Upon the souls of those, and they are very few,
Who strive to know where wisdom flows...

Don't let me cling
To the memories of one dream
A little death of self.
Let me be immersed
In the fragrance of the moment
And the promise of eternity.

I sew my life with threads of gold
The gods above will stare in awe!
And wonder at this splendor.

Soul is calling me back
Away from the world of desire
Away from the world of thoughts.

The events in your life will all pass
Like clouds across the sky.
Don't hang on to clouds
Stay true to who you really are-
The eternal sky beyond.

In stillness and in silence
Lie all the answers
Of your wavering mind.

My life lays marks for me follow
And has grandiose designs
But I fall behind
Distracted by the butterflies!

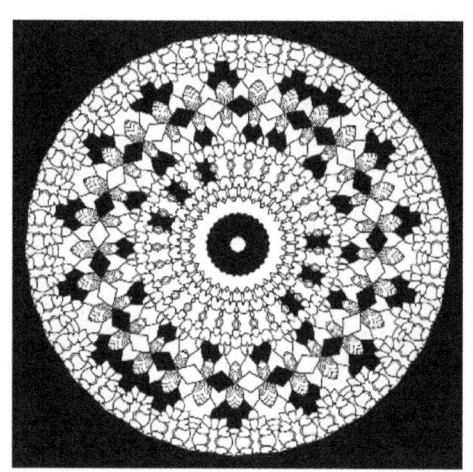

In the breeze, his love whispers
With rain he caresses my face
Sun's rays, his warm embrace
In the night, my body stirred
My lover needs no words.

The stars above look down in wonder
This miraculous game
Of human glory and of blunder.

Under the buddha tree,
Silence gathers in lovely garlands.

Somber thoughts, like dark clouds across my mind
Let some raindrops to fertilize my ground
Of creativity.

Rainbow gifts and cosmic thrills
Replies of silent whispers to my heart's affairs
Shaping reality with artist skills
Creating beauty beyond compare.
Master of mist and smoke.
With timeless grace
Immerse this dream with such fragrance of immortal soul,
My heart drunk
Follows this bliss all the way home
And needs no more.

Sky, whisper to me, please
The secret
Of the whirling snowflake.

Brilliant, multifaceted diamond!
So rare, precious and hard
Nothing can break you apart!
Won't you please
Replace my tender heart?

No eyes will ever see
The exquisite dance you make
Tiny snowflake,
Twirling to the ground.

So much unspoken beauty
Lost,
In between these spoken words.

Flow, river Soul, flow back home
And carry nothing with you,
Let it all go.

Dance with me, death, I have no fear
Of your cold embrace
A brief encounter in the boundlessness of time,
We're well acquainted, let us be chums.

I am nothing but the echo
Of my whispering soul.

Give me back my children's vision
To see the world anew,
Colored pebbles and playful butterflies!
That timeless age that this soul knew.

I lay my head on a pillow of silence
And swim the ocean of knowingness.

We pierce the fabric of time
Like birds piercing the sky-
Leaving no traces.
What is there to cling to?

Watch the river, Soul, and learn to flow
Heart, be solid like the stone
Mind, reflect the restful lake
Nature lays the path to take.

My hidden Self, a nameless Amazon
Frightful and uncharted
Calls an alluring song
To share its hidden gemstones.

From stony stillness and single oneness
Expanding,
Such is the breath of creation, and of the universe
To motion and infinite complexity
A feast to keep the eye enchanted
And the mind entangled
For many spiraling lives
Then contracting
Back to one again.

Life is ephemeral
And find its meaning
In its traceless flight.

I see my face reflected
In the heights of the towering skies
As in the tiny morning dew.

Treading into unknown lands
And leaving you behind, words
You are useless where I want to go.

I escort life, I partner death
They come and go.
Two visitors, I treat them well
They bring me gifts,
Life brings my joy, death brings me rest.
I only watch, to neither am I attached.

My soul carries the fragrance
Of an eternal time
This, my existence sublime.

The willow bends with the wind
I yield to life's sway
And never break.

The world speaks to me
Not in words or sounds
But in silences profound.

We come into the world
As babes protected by the womb
Surrounded by angelic light
Nourished and bound by mystic cords
And sustained with adoration
By heavenly delight.
And we proceed upon creation
To break away and proclaim our separation
And deny our sacred birth
Walk the earth with hollow eyes
Blind, and void of mirth,
Authors of our own demise.

The butterfly doesn't question
The purpose of its wings
And so creates its flight.

Blossoms of inspiration
Are sown
In moments of silence.

My mind measures time in days
And suffers in enduring poverty,
My heart beats in the spontaneous now
And has eternity for company.

The moon shares her full splendor
With the dreamers and the story tellers,
Secrets uncovered and truths disrobed
In the light of the silver orb.

Truth is a song that vibrates deep in the heart
And makes a melody of life.

Chirping birds, blossoming flowers
My heart replies with impetuous ardor
And longs to join this natural glee
And be the butterfly among the trees.

This life, an ephemeral dream
Holds nothing in esteem
Not love, not death, not time.
Its unfathomable origination
A mere playground of creation.

Removing veils, one by one
Making pathways
To return home.

Angels are light and soar high
For there is nothing holding them down.

Little butterfly, to his surprise,
His long slumber gave rise
To his wondrous flight!

I tiptoe through life
Leaving no traces
Creating a song
That remains unheard.

Wretched time, eats at my skin
Devouring my beauty!
But you cannot affect this soul
It will outlast you all in all
And will engulf you in eternity.

Hold out your hand, Soul
We have a long way to go
This path does not end
As long as you cry
"I want more, I want more!"

An intricate tapestry is life
Each moment, meeting and phenomenon
A wonderous pattern of its own,
In many loves, desires, and dreams we sew
Inscrutable designs
Impossible for mind to apprehend
Such complexity of divine intent,
A work to be completed and beheld in awe.

Strokes of color, and music tones
The canvas of my life adorns
And make this dream delightful.
But to what end, all this diversion?
Surrender into emptiness,
Let the silences behind
Surround you.

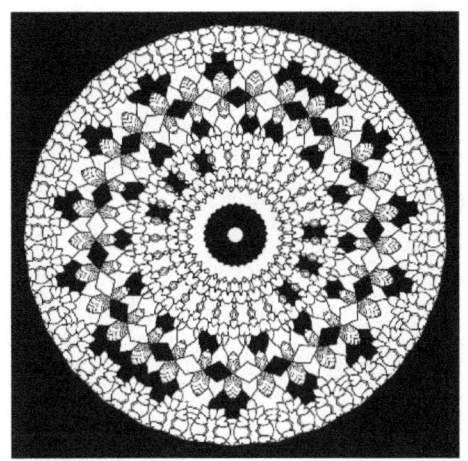

This dream, like floating mist
Is slipping though my fingers.

Fleeting moment, sing me the song
Of your eternal nature
Alas, I fail to remember!

Mirror above, mirror below
You show my face, I reflect your soul
Arising, unexpected laughter.
What curious game of hide and seek
Is this we play?

The blue of your sky in the shade of my eye
The change of your seasons in pace with my rhythm,
My gloom, reflected in your darkness
My joy, in your brightness
My death gives rest to your breath.
Life, why did you not say, your soul and mine
Are One and the same?

Give in the phantom dream
I hold nothing in esteem
I keep nothing of my own.
Take away my paper face,
Remove my vapor body,
I'll be an echo of your thoughts
A dancer on your fancy.

Don't be troubled, little cocoon,
Your truth is yet to be unravelled.

Chained in dreams of love and pain
And multiplicity of names
Deceiving Maya,
Stop your deluding game!
I want to see my One true face.

Vibration of creation
Still echoes in the caves of my soul.
Who can translate your secret song
And fathom the mystery of Om?

Each life, a momentary flutter
On this eternal journey-
Our flight to infinity.

Leaving traces of poem pebbles
For the universe to follow
My footsteps of desire
To my soul home.

Surface upwards, buried memories of truth,
So many lives travelled in vain
My body shaped in many forms,
I can't remember my original name.

Between me and my chosen goal
Lies my restless mind
That awaits
To be melted into love.

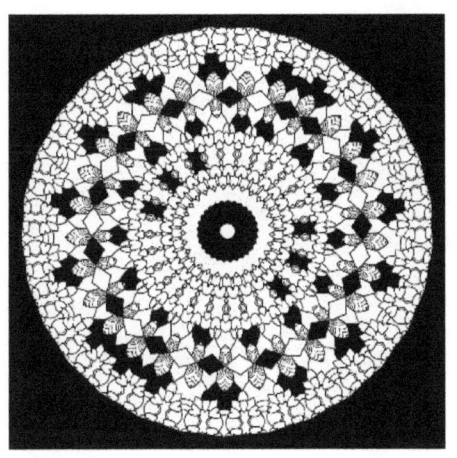

This life, my fear and my saviour
You are what I am looking for,
You are what I am running from,
There is no escape
From this
My own face.

From mineral, to plant and animal
And to noble human,
The breath of consciousness evolves
In seeming time
And climbs the ladder of creation
To meet its divine origination.

A spark, of thought divine,
Enough to start
The makings of creation
And commence the dance
Of life and death…

Lustrous silence offers
Windows into eternity.

On the heights of laughter
We build bridges between heaven and earth.

See my face! A thousand petaled-lotus
Rooted deep in murky matter
My splendor beauty yet untouched
Adorned, by precious jewel in the center
A clear and unclouded mind
To pierce through the illusion-life
With the purity of its refined sight.

Going in, going out
This breath now holds our only truth.
A bridge between two worlds
Separated by illusion
An outer and an inner world
Arising from within.
My breath, my life commander
The cord that bonds mind to matter
My anchor in eternity.

My soul's incessant yearning
To cross
The river of forgetfulness
And dive in divine discerning.

This life, a fleeting sigh
In an ocean of remembrance
Of soaring laughter
Of abysmal sorrow.

I see the world through million eyes,
Those suffering souls, these aching hearts
Mellow, carefree children's laughter
Are all my own.
Those leaning trees, feel them sway
Look! flying birds and falling rain
Running beasts, rushing streams, ocean waves-
My very face.
In all the places
Through all the eyes
I am the eternal seer.
I am the oversoul,
I am the One behind the many,
I am the One behind the all.

Moonflower, so rare, mysterious and unexpected
You sing your song alone,
I could not love you any more.

Within me, I hold immortality
Within me, I hold mortality
Looking at the sky above I embrace infinity,
Looking at the ground, I see my limits
I am the end, and the beginning,
I am all that can behold.

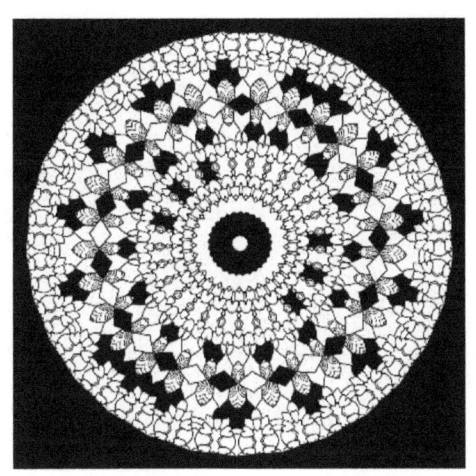

Choiceless births begin again.
Caught in paradox of highs and lows
With vision clouded by merciless veils
And temptations to derail
And fear of deathless death.
They don't know under their feet
Lie circles of infinity.

Behind the form, the formless
Behind the named, the nameless
Behind the multiplicity, the One
Gives birth to all and none.

Delicate butterfly flutters
Enough to set in motion
Such ripples of commotion
And cosmic consequence.

Out of nebulous beginnings
My body born, of cosmic dust
My soul alone belongs to god
My mind, a slave to time.

On my soul's eternal journey
I lay my head down in a little rest
With inevitable company
My old friend, death.

The light that gives the breath's delight
Now hid behind these sleeping eyes
We are pale shadows in the game of life.
Forsaken memory, awaken!
From perfect stillness
You emerged, in many cosmic splendors
Oh, those are lucky who remember!
I can do no better favour
Than submit to sweet surrender
And allow this Highest Will
Play out its Wonder.

Every life we walk in footprints
Of past lives gone,
Every moment we play an echo
Of yesterday's song.

About the Author

As a child growing up in Romania, I was captivated by a popular children's story about a penguin named "Apolodor" who lived in Labrador. While this innocent little story made me dream of the rugged Canadian wilderness, I never imagined that my father (a geologist) would relocate our family to Newfoundland and Labrador during my teens. The Canadian culture, not to mention the intoxicating and pristine land, opened me to new ideas that were utterly unknown to my life in Romania.

During this time, I stumbled across a dusty, old yoga book and felt an immediate, strong connection. I diligently taught myself the postures while following the book's focus on fitness and flexibility. However, I soon realized that those strange exercises were opening me to something unexpected—something beyond the mere physical. As I learned more about the philosophy behind yoga, I became mesmerized by the incredible stories of Indian yogis, with their mystical powers and their outlandish ideas of life and rebirth that made more sense than anything I had ever heard.

It's been nearly thirty years later, and I still continue my self-directed yoga practice. During the past ten years or so, this has included meditation, which has played a paramount role in my adult life. By silencing the 'monkey mind,' I have learned to access spaces that are free from self-identification. There, I can feel, and sometimes glean knowledge from what appears to be an inexhaustible ocean of intuitive inspiration that feels 'true.'

As more insights started arriving from these spaces, I decided to scribble them on paper, in a manner akin to a dream journal. My musings eventually took the form of poems, which, thanks to the encouragement of friends and family, I am sharing with you now, even though I sometimes feel I'm more like their conduit rather than their author.

I sincerely hope my Butterfly Flutters make you feel as light-hearted and inspired as I felt when they arrived to me.

www.ingramcontent.com/pod-product-compliance
Lightning Source LLC
Chambersburg PA
CBHW020303090426
42735CB00009B/1198